D1607336

Learn My Language! Spanish

Spanish Words at the Park

By Johanna Leigh

Gareth Stevens
Publishing

Please visit our website, www.garethstevens.com. For a free color catalog of all our high-quality books, call toll free 1-800-542-2595 or fax 1-877-542-2596.

Library of Congress Cataloging-in-Publication Data

Leigh, Johanna.
Spanish words at the park / by Johanna Leigh.
 p. cm. — (Learn my language! Spanish)
Includes index.
ISBN 978-1-4824-0345-9 (pbk.)
ISBN 978-1-4824-0349-7 (6-pack)
ISBN 978-1-4824-0346-6 (library binding)
1. Parks — Juvenile literature. 2. Parks — Recreational use — Juvenile literature. 3. Spanish language — Vocabulary — Juvenile literature. I. Title.
PC4129.E5 L45 2014
468—dc23

First Edition

Published in 2014 by
Gareth Stevens Publishing
111 East 14th Street, Suite 349
New York, NY 10003

Copyright © 2014 Gareth Stevens Publishing

Designer: Sarah Liddell
Editor: Therese Shea

Photo credits: Cover, p. 1 Jo Ann Snover/Shutterstock.com; p. 5 Monkey Business Images/Shutterstock.com; p. 7 Artens/Shutterstock.com; p. 9 LaNae Christenson/Shutterstock.com; p. 11 © iStockphoto.com/chuckcollier; p. 13 Rob Marmion/Shutterstock.com; p. 15 © iStockphoto.com/sykadelx; p. 17 bikeriderlondon/Shutterstock.com; p. 19 © iStockphoto.com/RonTech2000; p. 21 spotmatik/Shutterstock.com.

Printed in the United States of America

CPSIA compliance information: Batch #CW14GS: For further information contact Gareth Stevens, New York, New York at 1-800-542-2595.

Contents

Boldface words appear in the glossary.

Español at the Park

We're going to the park today. Let's learn some Spanish words there. *Español* is the word for Spanish. The Spanish word for park is *parque*. Look in the box on each page to learn how to say the Spanish words.

Spanish = español (ehs-pah-NYOHL)

park = parque (PAHR-kay)

parque

5

The Garden

Our park has a colorful garden. The Spanish word for garden is *jardín*. The *jardín* is full of beautiful flowers, or *flores*. The *flores* smell so good!

garden = jardín (har-DEEN)

flowers = flores (FLOH-rehs)

flores

7

Let's Swing

Our park has a playground. In Spanish, playground is *parque infantil*. The swings are my favorite part. The Spanish word for swings is *columpios*.

playground = parque infantil
         (PAHR-Kay een-fahn-TEEL)

swings = columpios (koh-LUM-pyohs)

columpios

9

Seesaw

Let's go on the seesaw next. The Spanish word for seesaw is *subibaja*. We go up and down until we're very *cansados*. That's Spanish for tired.

---

seesaw = subibaja (soo-bee-BAH-ha)

tired = cansados (kahn-SAH-dohs)

subibaja

11

Slippery Slide

The slide is fun. It's called a *resbaladilla* in Spanish. The *resbaladilla* is steep and **slippery**. That makes it *rápida*! That's the Spanish word for fast.

slide = resbaladilla (rehs-bah-lah-DEE-yah)

fast = rápida (RRA-pee-dah)

resbaladilla

The Duck Pond

The park has an *estanque*. That's Spanish for pond. The *estanque* has ducks in it. The Spanish word for ducks is *patos*. How many *patos* do you see?

pond = estanque (ehs-TAHN-keh)

ducks = patos (PAH-tohs)

estanque

patos

15

A Picnic

We packed a **picnic** lunch. Lunch is *almuerzo* in Spanish. The park has a table, or *mesa*, where we can eat. There are lots of tasty things to eat on the *mesa*!

lunch = almuerzo (ahl-MWEHR-soh)

table = mesa (MEH-sah)

mesa

Monkey Bars

Let's run over to the monkey bars. The Spanish word for monkey bars is *pasamanos*. Our hands, or *manos*, hold tight as we swing from one side to another. Don't fall!

monkey bars = pasamanos
(pah-sah-MAH-nohs)

hands = manos (MAH-nohs)

pasamanos

19

Buenas Noches

It's getting late. We say *buenas noches* to the friends we made. That means "good night." The park was *divertido*! That's Spanish for fun. Maybe we'll come back tomorrow!

good night = buenas noches
(BWEH-nahs NOH-chehs)

fun = divertido (dee-ber-TEE-doh)

Glossary

picnic: a meal made for eating outside

slippery: causing someone to slide or slip easily

For More Information

Books

Acosta, Tatiana, and Guillermo Gutiérrez. *Things at the Park/ Las Cosas del Parque*. Milwaukee, WI: Weekly Reader Early Learning Library, 2007.

Gorman, Jacqueline Laks. *The Playground/El Parque*. Milwaukee, WI: Weekly Reader Early Learning Library, 2005.

Stanley, Mandy. *In the Park/Vamos al Parque*. Boston, MA: Kingfisher, 2004.

Websites

Merriam-Webster Spanish-English Dictionary
www.merriam-webster.com/spanish/
Find a Spanish word you don't know? Look it up in this online dictionary.

Primary Spanish
www.bbc.co.uk/schools/primaryspanish/start_here/
Learn some important Spanish phrases.

Index